The future belongs to those who believe in the beauty of their dreams.

— Marie Curie

Blue Mountain Arts®

New and Best-Selling Titles

By Susan Polis Schutz:
To My Daughter with Love on the Important Things in Life
To My Son with Love

By Douglas Pagels:
For You, My Soul Mate
100 Things to Always Remember... and One Thing to Never Forget
Required Reading for All Teenagers

By Marci:
Friends Are Forever
10 Simple Things to Remember
To My Daughter
You Are My "Once in a Lifetime"

By Wally Amos, with Stu Glauberman:
The Path to Success Is Paved with Positive Thinking

By M. Butler and D. Mastromarino:
Take Time for You

By James Downton, Jr.:
Today, I Will... Words to Inspire Positive Life Changes

By Donna Fargo:
I Thanked God for You Today

Anthologies:
A Daughter Is Life's Greatest Gift
A Sister's Love Is Forever
A Son Is Life's Greatest Gift
Dream Big, Stay Positive, and Believe in Yourself
Friends for Life
God Is Always Watching Over You
Hang In There
Keep Believing in Yourself and Your Dreams
The Love Between a Mother and Daughter Is Forever
The Strength of Women
Think Positive Thoughts Every Day
Words Every Woman Should Remember

Always *Believe* in *Yourself* and Your *Dreams*

A Blue Mountain Arts® Collection

Edited by Patricia Wayant

Blue Mountain Press™
Boulder, Colorado

Library of Congress Control Number: 2012953840
ISBN: 978-1-59842-703-5

◼ and Blue Mountain Press are registered in U.S. Patent and Trademark Office.
Certain trademarks are used under license.

Printed in China.
First Printing: 2013

Blue Mountain Arts, Inc.
P.O. Box 4549, Boulder, Colorado 80306

Contents

Always Believe in Yourself and Your Dreams

Dreams can come true
if you take the time to
think about what you want in life
Get to know yourself
Find out who you are
Choose your goals carefully
Be honest with yourself
Always believe in yourself
Find many interests and pursue them
Find out what is important to you
Find out what you are good at
Don't be afraid to make mistakes
Work hard to achieve successes

When things are not going right
don't give up — just try harder
Give yourself freedom to try out new things
Laugh and have a good time
Open yourself up to love
Take part in the beauty of nature
Be appreciative of all that you have
Help those less fortunate than you
Work toward peace in the world
Live life to the fullest
Create your own dreams and
follow them until they are a reality

— Susan Polis Schutz

Your Life Holds Unlimited Potential

You have the ability
to attain whatever you seek;
within you is every potential
you can imagine.
Always aim higher than
you believe you can reach.
So often, you'll discover
that when your talents
are set free by your imagination,
you can achieve any goal.
If people offer their help or wisdom
as you go through life,
accept it gratefully.
You can learn much from those
who have gone before you.

Never be afraid or hesitant
to step off the accepted path
and head in your own direction
if your heart tells you
that it's the right way for you.
Always believe that you will
ultimately succeed
at whatever you do,
and never forget the value
of persistence, discipline,
and determination.
You are meant to be
whatever you dream
of becoming.

— Edmund O'Neill

One Step at a Time

Every goal that has ever been reached
began with just one step —
and the belief that
it could be attained.

Dreams really can come true,
but they are most often the result
of hard work, determination,
    and persistence.

When the end of the journey
seems impossible to reach,
remember that all you need to do
is take one more step.

Stay focused on your goal
and remember...
each small step will bring you
   a little closer.

When the road becomes
   hard to travel
and it feels as if you'll never
   reach the end...
look deep inside your heart
and you will find strength
   you never knew you had.

— Jason Blume

You're on the Journey of a Lifetime...

A journey no one else will travel and no one else can judge — a path of happiness and hurt, where the challenges are great and the rewards even greater. You're on a journey where each experience will teach you something valuable and you can't get lost, for you already know the way by heart.

You're on a journey that is universal yet uniquely personal, and profound yet astonishingly simple — where sometimes you will stumble and other times you will soar. You'll learn that even at your darkest point you can find a light — if you look for it. At the most difficult crossroad, you'll have an answer — if you listen for it. Friends and family will accompany you part of the way, and you'll walk the rest by yourself... but you will never be alone.

Travel at your own pace. There'll be time enough to learn all you need to know and go as far as you're meant to go. Travel light. Letting go of extra baggage will keep your arms open and your heart free to fully embrace the gifts of the moment.

You may not always know exactly where you're headed, but if you follow the desires of your heart, the integrity of your conscience, and the wisdom of your soul... then each step you take will lead you to discover more of who you really are, and it will be a step in the right direction on the journey of a lifetime.

— Paula Finn

You Can Be Whatever You Want to Be

Be yourself, believe in yourself, try to love everything about yourself... and you'll be respected. ❧ Take care of your body and continue to challenge your mind... and you'll be admired. ❧ Don't listen to anyone who questions your dreams or your choices. ❧ Be your own leader... and others will follow you. ❧ Make the most of every moment, embrace every opportunity, and take lots of pictures... There's so much you'll want to remember. ❧ Take chances, trust your instincts, and celebrate every achievement — big or small. ❧ But most importantly, never give up on your dreams, because... you're going to love your future.

— Charley Knox

Your dreams can take you... to the corners of your smiles, to the highest of your hopes, to the windows of your opportunities, and to the most special places your heart has ever known.

— Carson Wrenn

Believe that you can, and you will. Imagine yourself to be the type of person you want to be, and then be it. You may have to let go of some bad habits and develop some new ones, but don't give up — for it is only in trying and persisting that dreams come true.

Expect changes to occur, and realize that the power to make those changes comes from within you. Your thoughts and actions, the way you spend your time, your choices and decisions determine who you are and who you will become.

You are capable and worthy of being and doing anything. You just need the discipline and determination to see it through. It won't come instantly, and you may backslide from time to time, but don't let that deter you. Never give up.

— Barbara Cage

Make Choices That Are Right for You

Remember that no one can ever
make your choices for you.
What you do with your life
    is your own choice.
How you decide to live your life
    and achieve your goals is up to you,
        and no one but you.
Those who may at first disagree
    will, in time, be happy for you too.
Then you will come to see
    that the choices you make are right —
        if you make them for yourself.

— Jodi R. Ernst

It is so important
to choose your own
lifestyle
and not let others
choose it for you

— Susan Polis Schutz

Decisions are incredibly important things!
Good decisions will come back to bless you.
Bad decisions can come back to haunt you.

That's why it's so important that you take
the time to choose wisely.

Choose to do the things that will reflect
well... on your ability, your integrity, your
spirit, your health, your tomorrows, your
smiles, your dreams, and yourself.

There is someone who will thank you for doing the things you do now with foresight and wisdom and respect.

It's the person you will someday be.

You have a chance to make that person so thankful and so proud. All you have to do is remember these nine little words:

Each time you come to a crossroads
...choose wisely.
— Douglas Pagels

Take a Chance
Now and Then

If we don't ever take chances,
    we won't reach the rainbows.
If we don't ever search,
    we'll never be able to find.
If we don't attempt to get over
    our doubts and fears,
        we'll never discover how wonderful
           it is to live without them.
If we don't go beyond difficulty,
    we won't grow any stronger.
If we don't keep our dreams alive,
    we won't have our dreams any longer.

But...
if we can take a chance now and then,
seek and search, discover and dream,
grow and go through each day
with the knowledge that
we can only take as much as we can give
and we can only get as much out of life
     as we allow ourselves to live...

Then...
we can be truly happy.
We can realize a dream or two along the way,
and we can make a habit of
     reaching out for rainbows
          and coloring our lives
               with wonderful days.
                         — Collin McCarty

Dare to reach out
for the things no one else can see.
Be unafraid to see what others cannot.
Believe in your heart
    and in your own goodness,
for in doing so
    others will believe in them too.
Believe in magic,
    because life is full of it.
But most of all,
    believe in yourself...
because within you lies
    all the magic, the hope, the love,
and the dreams of tomorrow.

— Ron Cristian

Have the daring to accept yourself as a bundle of possibilities and undertake the game of making the most of your best.

— Henry Emerson Fosdick

Only those who will risk going too far can possibly find out how far one can go.

— T. S. Eliot

Keep Moving Forward

When the road curves
to lead you into new discoveries...
let it take you.
When the wind pulls
    under your wings
and urges you on to greater heights...
let it take you...
When the page you're on
    builds suspense, turn it —
for it will end happily.
Let it take you there.

The journey of life
  has no blueprints.
You find it as you grow
through prayer, joy,
pain, and love.
Keep moving on your path,
keep learning and trying
for the good and the best —
and it will take you there.

— Susan A. J. Lyttek

We grow great by dreams.
Dreamers... see things
in the soft haze of a spring day
or in the red fire
of a long winter's evening.
Some of us let these great dreams die,
but others nourish and protect them,
nurse them through bad days
till they bring them to
the sunshine and light
which comes always to those
who sincerely hope that
their dreams will come true.

— Woodrow Wilson

You can have many dreams —
of living a life that you design
of earning a living at what you like to do
of finding the perfect person
     to share your life with
of always remaining vigorous and healthy
of having a good time every day
of always being around beautiful things
Even if everything you dream about
     does not always come true
it is still important to dream
because the more you pursue your dreams
the greater the chance your dreams have
of coming true

— Susan Polis Schutz

Be True to Yourself

Seek out that particular mental attribute which makes you feel most deeply and vitally alive, along with which comes the inner voice that says, "This is the real me," and when you have found that attitude, follow it.

— William James

Always be yourself... for no one else can compare to the integrity of your own heart... and nothing can compare to your spirit, your style, your smile, your laughter.

— Ashley Rice

No matter what you undertake in life, do so with a joyful and positive attitude. Work hard and try your best, pouring your heart into all you do. Demonstrate sincere gratitude and don't take your loved ones for granted. Don't just "follow the crowd," take a firm stand in maintaining your individuality.

— Debbie Burton-Peddle

I believe all of us have a built-in compass to help us get to wherever we desire to go. Don't forget to trust that compass, and refer to it often, for with that trusting will come the strength to bear whatever life deals you.

Don't get led astray. Ask your heart for the truth, and it will come up with the answer and the good judgment to make the decisions you'll need to make. Love everyone, and don't question love's reception. Do the best you can. Live each day as it comes. We can't get ahead of ourselves anyway.

Remember: just as you have questions now, somewhere inside you, and down the road, there will be better answers and workable solutions. It takes patience and trust to get through life's changes when you're trying to reach goals, solve problems, and make dreams come true. Though at times it may seem more than you can take, you are strong, and you can handle whatever comes your way. Trust in yourself.

— Donna Fargo

Don't Be Discouraged by Failure

Failure can be a positive experience. It is, in a sense, the highway to success, inasmuch as every discovery of what is false leads us to seek earnestly after what is true.

— John Keats

Our greatest glory is not in never failing, but in rising up every time we fail.

— Ralph Waldo Emerson

There are times in every life
when we feel hurt or alone...
But I believe that these times
when we feel lost and all around us
    seems to be falling apart
are really bridges of growth.
We struggle and try to recapture
    the security of what was,
but almost in spite of ourselves,
    we emerge on the other side
with a new understanding,
    a new awareness, a new strength.
It is almost as though we must
go through the pain and the struggle
in order to grow and reach
    new heights.

— Sue Mitchell

Sometimes you may
think that you
need to be perfect
that you cannot
make mistakes
At these times
you put so much
pressure on yourself
Try to realize
that you are
like everyone else —
capable of
reaching great potential
but not capable of
being perfect

Just do your best
and realize that
this is enough
Don't compare yourself
to anyone
Be happy to be
the wonderful
unique, very special
person that you are

— Susan Polis Schutz

Answers Will Come

Sometimes, we are overwhelmed
    with the obstacles
we are given in our lives,
and we ask, "Why me?"
And often, when the answers elude us,
we believe that the trials
through which we suffer
are unfair and harsh.
But there are answers, even though we
    may not recognize them.

In this world, we are all connected
and there is a reason for whatever happens.
We must remain strong in the
    face of adversity
and meet the challenges one day at a time.
And as time heals us, both body and soul,
we may come to understand the meaning
    of our trials
and recognize the good that came from them.
We may take pride in knowing that we
    made it through them,
and as a result are much stronger
than we were before.

— Judith Mammay

When your dreams seem far away,
hang in there and have patience
with yourself.
Live in the moment,
not fretting about the past
   or worrying about the future.
Don't take on more than you have to;
learn to let go.
Refuse negative thoughts;
replace them with positive ones.

Look for the good things in your life
and make a point of appreciating them.
You are ultimately the one
    in charge of your life
and the only person in the world
    who can change it.
No matter how much others
    are pulling for you
or how much anyone else cares,
<u>you</u> must do what needs to be done
to make your present and future
everything you want it to be.

— Barbara Cage

Listen to the Voice
Deep Inside You

As the dawn of each morning
peers into your life,
there lies a path to follow.
Delicate whispers can be heard
if you listen to the sound of your heart
and the voice that speaks within you.
If you listen closely to your soul,
you will become aware of your dreams
that are yet to unfold.
You will discover that there lies within you
a voice of confidence and strength
that will prompt you to seek a journey
and live a dream.

Within the depths of your mind,
the purpose and direction of your life
can be determined by listening intently
to the knowledge that you already possess.
Your heart, mind, and soul
are the foundation
of your success and happiness.

In the still of each passing moment,
may you come to understand that
you are capable of reaching a higher destiny.
When you come to believe in all that you are
and all that you can become,
there will be no cause for doubt.
Believe in your heart, for it offers hope.
Believe in your mind, for it offers direction.
Believe in your soul, for it offers strength.
But above all else... believe in yourself.

— Leslie Neilson

Keep looking forward to the future... to all you might be. Don't let old mistakes or misfortunes hold you down: learn from them, forgive yourself — or others — and move on. Do not be bothered or discouraged by adversity. Instead, meet it as a challenge. Be empowered by the courage it takes you to overcome obstacles. Learn something new every day. Be interested in others and what they might teach you, but do not look for yourself in other people's approval.

As far as who you are and who you will become goes... the answer is always within yourself. Believe in yourself. Follow your heart and your dreams. You, like everyone, will make mistakes. But so long as you are true to the strength within your own heart... you can never go wrong.

— Ashley Rice

It's Up to You to Make Your Life the Best It Can Be

This life is the only one you're given.
Look for opportunities to grow,
and never be discouraged
in your efforts to do so.
Replace your weaknesses with positives;
take life's broken pieces
and re-create your dreams.
Never measure the future by the past;
let yesterday become a memory
and tomorrow a promise.

Begin each day by focusing
on all that is good,
and you'll be in a position
to handle whatever comes along.
Take responsibility for your actions;
never make excuses for not being
the best you can be.
If you should slip,
be comforted by the thought
that we all do at times.
Determine your tomorrow
by the choices you make today,
and you'll find yourself living
in joy and triumph.

— Linda E. Knight

You have everything you need to take you
    where you want to go.
You have abilities and talents and attributes
    that belong to you alone, and you have what
    it takes to make your path of success lead
    to happiness.
You have qualities that get better every day!
You have the courage and strength to see things
    through.
You have smiles that will serve as your guides.
You have a light that will shine in you till the
    end of time.

You have known the truth of yesterday,
   and you have an inner map that
   will lead the way to a very beautiful
   tomorrow.
You have gifts that have never even been
   opened and personal journeys waiting
   to be explored. You have so much
   going for you.
You are a special person, and you have a
   future that is in the best of hands.
   And you need to remember: if you have
   plans you want to act on and dreams
   you've always wanted to come true...

You have what it takes, because...
   You have you.
                              — Douglas Pagels

Aim for the Stars

All who have accomplished
    great things
have had a great aim
and fixed their gaze
on a goal which was high —
one which sometimes seemed
    impossible.

— Orison Swett Marden

Remember that a wish
can take you anywhere —
and half the fun is reaching for a star.
Your dreams were made to soar;
let your spirit dance
in every waking moment.
Every day comes bearing gifts;
hold each promise in your hands.
Within you is your very own universe.
A bit of stardust is blowing your way —
a bit of light and a bit of wonder.
Follow your leanings;
listen to the whispers of your soul.

— Linda E. Knight

Imagine... Here you are, on the high peak of a mountain. You can choose to wing your way toward the clouds, or you can simply walk the usual, ordinary paths that lead to the valley below.

Which choice will you make —
the well-worn paths or rising above it all?

Beautiful things await you
if you can reach the heights.

— George Sand

We must never be afraid to go too far, for success lies just beyond.

— Marcel Proust

Twenty years from now you will be more disappointed by the things that you didn't do than by the ones you did do. So throw off the bowlines. Catch the trade winds in your sails. Explore. Dream. Discover.

— Mark Twain

It Takes Strength and Courage

Sometimes you fight your way
through battle after battle
and show your strength and courage
by being a warrior.
You wait, listen to your heart,
find wisdom to take the right path,
and show your strength and courage
by being patient.
You stand up
for what you believe in,
say "no" to that which is not
compatible with your values,
and show your strength and courage
by being true to yourself.

You open new doors for yourself
even when you seem too tired to go on.
You find the energy to see a new dawn —
a new point of view —
and create a new direction
where none seems possible.
You show your strength and courage
by being optimistic.
No matter how many times
you are knocked down,
you continue to rise again.

— Bonnie St. John

You are stronger than you think —
remember to stand tall.
Every challenge in your life
helps you to grow.
Every problem you encounter
strengthens your mind and your soul.
Every trouble you overcome
increases your understanding of life.

— Lisa Wroble

Be so strong that nothing can disturb your peace of mind. Talk health, happiness, and prosperity to every person you meet. Make all your friends feel there is something in them. Look at the sunny side of everything. Think only of the best, work only for the best, and expect only the best. Be as enthusiastic about the success of others as you are about your own. Forget the mistakes of the past and press on to the greater achievements of the future. Give everyone a smile. Spend so much time improving yourself that you have no time left to criticize others. Be too big for worry and too noble for anger.

— Christian D. Larsen

Your Hard Work Will Be Rewarded

The path to a dream is paved
      with sacrifices
and lined with determination.
And though it has many stumbling blocks
      along the way
and may go in more than one direction,
      it is marked with faith.
It is traveled by belief and courage,
      persistence and hard work.

It is conquered with a willingness
to face challenges and take chances,
   to fail and try again and again.
Along the way, you may have to confront
   doubts, setbacks, and unfairness.
But when the path comes to an end,
you will find that there is no greater joy
than making your dream come true.

— Barbara Cage

People Who Achieve Their Dreams Have Twelve Qualities in Common

They have confidence in themselves
They have a very strong sense of purpose
They never have excuses for not doing something
They always try their hardest for perfection
They never consider the idea of failing
They work extremely hard toward their goals
They know who they are

They understand their weaknesses
as well as their strong points
They can accept and benefit from criticism
They know when to defend what they are doing
They are creative
They are not afraid to be a little different
in finding innovative solutions
that will enable them to achieve their dreams

— Susan Polis Schutz

Think You Can!

You have powers you never dreamed of. You can do things you never thought you could do. There are no limitations in what you can do except the limitations in your own mind as to what you cannot do.

Don't think you cannot.

Think you can.

— Darwin P. Kingsley

You can do anything if you have enthusiasm.

— Henry Ford

Clear your mind of can't.

— Samuel Johnson

Catch the star that holds your destiny —
the one that forever twinkles
within your heart
Take advantage of precious opportunities
while they still sparkle before you
Always believe that your ultimate goal
is attainable as long as you
commit yourself to it
Though barriers may sometimes
stand in the way of your dreams
remember that your destiny is hiding behind them
Accept the fact that not everyone
is going to approve of the choices you make
but have faith in your judgment

Catch the star that twinkles in your heart
and it will lead you to your destiny's path
Follow that pathway and uncover the
sweet sunrises that await you
Take pride in your accomplishments
as they are steppingstones to your dreams
Understand that you may make mistakes
but don't let them discourage you
Value your capabilities and talents
for they are what make you truly unique
The greatest gifts in life are not purchased
but acquired through hard work
and determination
Find the star that twinkles in your heart
for you are capable of making
your brightest dreams come true
Give your hopes everything you've got
and you will catch the star
that holds your destiny

— Shannon M. Dickinson

Don't Wait Another Day

Let nothing hold you back from
exploring your wildest fantasies,
    wishes, and aspirations.
Don't be afraid to dream big
and to follow your dreams
wherever they may lead you.
Open your eyes to their beauty;
open your mind to their magic;
open your heart to their
    possibilities.

Whether your dreams are in color
    or in black and white,
whether they are big or small,
    easily attainable or almost impossible,
look to your dreams
and make them become reality.
Wishes and hopes are nothing
until you take the first step
    toward making them something!
Only by dreaming
    will you ever discover
who you are, what you want,
    and what you can do.
                        — Julie Anne Ford

Ten Important Traveling Companions to Take with You on the Journey to Your Dreams

1. Confidence: for when things get tough, when you're overwhelmed, when you think of giving up.

2. Patience: with your own trials and temptations, and with others.

3. An adjustable attitude: one that doesn't react, but responds with well-thought-out actions and feelings.

4. Beauty: within yourself, in your surroundings, and in nature.

5. Excitement: new things to enjoy and learn and experience.

6. Fun: laughter and smiles any way you can get them.

7. Companionship: people to share your happiness and sorrows, your troubles and joys.

8. Health: mental, physical, and emotional.

9. Peace: with others, yourself, and in your environment.

10. Love: pure, unconditional, and eternal.

— Barbara Cage

There's No Challenge You Can't Face

Challenges make us stronger.
They push us to try harder.
They allow us to be brave.
They offer us courage.
They engender hope in us.
And sometimes we go farther
    than we ever dreamed possible...
        just by believing that we can.

When the task at hand
is a mountain in front of you,
it may seem too hard to climb.
But you don't have to climb it
all at once —
just one step at a time.
Take one small step...
and one small step...
then another...
and you'll find...
the task at hand that was
a mountain in front of you...

...is a mountain you have climbed.

— Ashley Rice

Even when you get a little discouraged, don't allow yourself to give up. Only when you have done your very best can you stop and say to yourself, "I tried," and that's what matters most.

If you back away from obstacles that appear before you because they seem too difficult, then you're not being true to yourself. Don't be afraid to take risks, or even to fail. It isn't about winning or losing. It's about loving yourself enough and believing in who you are that counts in the end.

Throughout your life, you will undoubtedly face challenges that may try your patience. Just remember that it is <u>you</u> who will always come out ahead, as long as you know in your heart that you did the best you could and that's all that really matters.

— T. L. Nash

Remember the Three Ps: Patience, Perseverance, and Purpose

Patience serves as a protection against wrongs as clothes do against cold. For if you put on more clothes as the cold increases, it will have no power to hurt you. So in like manner you must grow in patience when you meet with great wrongs, and they will then be powerless to vex your mind.

— Leonardo da Vinci

Perseverance is a great element of success. If you only knock long enough and loud enough at the gate, you are sure to wake up somebody.

— Henry Wadsworth Longfellow

A sense of purpose gives you the confidence to face each new day with boldness and courage.

— Cindy Chuksudoon

When you are in need of encouragement, remember that good things come to good people... and you're one of the best. Just hang in there and hold on. Your sun is still shining brightly in the sky up above, and it's just waiting for a break in the clouds... to shed its light on you.

When you are in search of hope, remember all the good things your tomorrows can bring.

When you are in need of understanding, know that somewhere someone does understand, and that you never have to feel alone.

When you are feeling uncertain about what to do or which way to go, remember that so many days are filled with decisions... but if you let your heart help you decide what is right for you, you will choose wisely.

When you are in need of patience and faith and strength, rely on all the good things that are available to you:
    inner peace, reaching out,
    steady goals, staying strong,
    and all your wonderful qualities
    that have always seen you through
    and that will continue to carry you on.

                                    — Douglas Pagels

Let Your Spirit Shine Through!

You have an inner jewel. Let your spirit, the divine gem, shine through, and create a radiance about you wherever you go.

Let your mind be planted with seeds of love and joy and hope, and courage and universal goodwill and opulent harvest shall grow.

Think of each year as a sower scattering these
seeds in your heart; then water them with
the dews of sympathy, and throw open the
windows to the broad sunlight of heaven while
they ripen.

And — as surely as the days come and go —
so surely shall your life grow.

— Ella Wheeler Wilcox

Set no barriers for yourself. Admit no barricades or obstacles. Anything in the way? Look at it, examine it, analyze your own relationship to the self-construction of it, clean up your own life and there will be an influx of that power to which there is no limit — unlimited you! You are unlimited! There is no limit for you!

— Dr. Preston Bradley

We can do whatever we wish to do provided our wish is strong enough.

— Katherine Mansfield

The golden opportunity you are seeking is in yourself. It is not in your environment; it is not in luck or chance, or the help of others; it is in yourself alone.

— Orison Swett Marden

Cultivate Confidence

If you know yourself well
and have developed a sense
of confidence in yourself
If you are honest with yourself
and honest with others
If you follow your heart
and adhere to your own truths
you are ready to share yourself
you are ready to set goals
you are ready to find happiness
And the more you love
and the more you give
and the more you feel
the more you will receive
from love
and the more you will receive
from life

— Susan Polis Schutz

Learn to trust your own capabilities. That might very well be the most important thing you ever learn. Hold tight to that confidence and to all you've discovered, as you set out on the road to your dreams. Get ready to meet your own greatness.

— Charley Knox

Self-confidence is the first requisite to great undertakings.

— Samuel Johnson

There may be days
when you get up in the morning
and things aren't the way
you had hoped they would be.
That's when you have to
tell yourself that things will get better.
There are times when people
disappoint you and let you down,
but those are the times
when you must remind yourself
to trust your own judgments and opinions,
to keep your life focused on
believing in yourself
and all that you are capable of.
There will be challenges to face
and changes to make in your life,
and it is up to you to accept them.

Constantly keep yourself headed
in the right direction for you.
It may not be easy at times,
but in those times of struggle,
you will find a stronger sense
    of who you are
and you will also see yourself
developing into the person
you have always wanted to be.

Life is a journey through time,
filled with many choices;
each of us will experience life
in our own special way.
So when the days come
that are filled with frustration
and unexpected responsibilities,
remember to believe in yourself
and all you want your life to be,
because the challenges and changes
will only help you to find
the dreams that you know
are meant to come true for you.

— Deanna Beisser

Don't Ever Lose Sight of the Wonderful Person You Are

Life can disappoint you sometimes, and things happen that you didn't expect and don't deserve. But you are an amazing person with beautiful dreams and wonderful gifts.

Don't ever downplay your abilities or your special charm. Keep living your life the best way you know how — with persistence, patience, and determination. Let go of the bad things and keep the good.

You are a remarkable person, and there is
so much ahead waiting for you: chances for
new adventures, possibilities you never even
dreamed of, and so many people who love you.

Take the time to rediscover yourself. Picture
what you want to come into your life. Choose
happiness. Believe in the wonderful person you
are and in your bright and shining future.

— Vickie M. Worsham

Reflect on all that you are and what you've achieved. The competition in the world is so great today, so every goal reached is something to be proud of. When all the elements come together to acknowledge someone's progress, it is truly something to celebrate.

Be inspired to continue doing the things that are important to you and to keep on making your dreams come true. Let the pride others have in you encourage you to continue to pursue your purpose.

— Donna Fargo

Give yourself all the credit you're due;
don't shortchange your qualities, your
abilities, or any of the things that are so
unique about you.

— Collin McCarty

Do not wish to be anything
but what you are,
and try to be that perfectly.

— St. Francis de Sales

Visualize Achieving Your Goal

You want a better position than you now have in business, a better and fuller place in life. All right; think of that better place and you in it as already existing. Form the mental image. Keep on thinking of that higher position, keep the image constantly before you, and — no, you will not suddenly be transported into the higher job, but you will find that you are preparing yourself to occupy the better position in life — your body, your energy, your understanding, your heart will all grow up to the job — and when you are ready, after hard work, after perhaps years of preparation, you will get the job and the higher place in life.

— Joseph H. Appel

Whatever you vividly imagine, ardently desire, sincerely believe, and enthusiastically act upon... must inevitably come to pass.

— Paul J. Meyer

If you can imagine it, you can achieve it; if you can dream it, you can become it.

— William Arthur Ward

Always bear in mind that your
own resolution to succeed is more
important than any one thing.

— Abraham Lincoln

To accomplish great things, we must
not only act, but also dream, not only
plan, but also believe.

— Anatole France

A thing that you sincerely believe in cannot be wrong.

— D. H. Lawrence

If we did all the things we are capable of, we would literally astound ourselves.

— Thomas A. Edison

Surround Yourself with People Who Support Your Dreams

Keep away from people who belittle your ambitions. Small people always do that, but the really great make you feel that you too can become great.

— Mark Twain

Surround yourself with those who believe in you and who will help you achieve your goals.

— Lisa Marie Yost

We don't make it alone in this world.
We're lucky that there are people
placed in our path to guide us,
protect us, and touch our lives
so that we can get through it all...
one day at a time.

— Julia Escobar

Ask for Help
If You Need It

Sometimes we do not feel
like we want to feel
Sometimes we do not achieve
what we want to achieve
Sometimes things happen
that do not make sense
Sometimes life leads us in directions
that are beyond our control
It is at these times most of all
that we need someone
who will quietly understand us
and be there to support us

— Susan Polis Schutz

You may think you are alone,
and you may feel as if
    you are just soldiering on.
But you couldn't be more wrong,
because you have a whole army
    of people behind you.
So the next time you feel alone
    with your problems
or feel downhearted in any way,
remember that army of supporters
    behind you —
people who care about you
    and are wishing you well.
May this thought help to keep you strong.

— Maria Mullins

Be Thankful
for All the Gifts
You've Been Given

Know in your heart that
you have the ability to become
all you are capable
of becoming.
Forget problems
that don't matter anymore
and worries that will wash away
on the shore of tomorrow.

Determine your own worth
by yourself,
and do not be dependent
on another's judgment of you.
Dare to dream,
and live those dreams,
for it is then
that you can begin to realize
your true destiny.
Live life fully
with thankfulness and joy
for all the gifts
you've been given.

— Debbi L. Oehman-Finke

Don't Let Go of Hope

Hope gives you the strength to keep going
when you feel like giving up.
Don't ever quit believing in yourself.
As long as you believe you can,
you will have a reason for trying.
Don't let anyone hold your happiness
    in their hands;
hold it in yours, so it will always be
    within your reach.
Don't measure success or failure by
    material wealth, but by how you feel;
our feelings determine the richness of
    our lives.
Don't let bad moments overcome you;
be patient, and they will pass.
Don't hesitate to reach out for help;
we all need it from time to time.
Don't run away from love
    but toward love,
because it is our deepest joy.

Don't wait for what you want
    to come to you.
Go after it with all that you are,
knowing that life will meet you halfway.
Don't feel like you've lost
when plans and dreams fall short of
    your hopes.
Anytime you learn something new
about yourself or about life,
you have progressed.
Don't do anything that takes away
from your self-respect.
Feeling good about yourself
is essential to feeling good about life.
Don't ever forget how to laugh
or be too proud to cry.
It is by doing both that we live life
    to its fullest.

— Nancye Sims

Follow Your Heart

Follow your heart;
never surrender your dreams.
Constantly work toward your goals.
Believe in yourself, and always be truthful.
Take time to enjoy life's pleasures.
Keep your mind open to new experiences.
Think before acting,
but don't forget the joys of spontaneity.
Make your own decisions.
Look out for yourself, but remember
that you share this universe with others.

— Melissa Ososki

The courage of working for
something you believe in,
day in and day out,
    year after year,
can be difficult
    but holds the greatest rewards.

Find your ideal...
    and follow it.

— V. Sukomlin

Hold Fast Your Dreams

Hold fast your dreams!
Within your heart,
Keep one still, secret spot
Where dreams may go,
And, sheltered so,
May thrive and grow
Where doubt and fear are not.
O keep a place apart,
Within your heart,
For little dreams to go!

We see so many ugly things —
Deceits and wrongs and quarrelings;
We know, alas! we know
How quickly fade
The color in the west,
The bloom upon the flower,
The bloom upon the breast,
And youth's blind hour.
Yet keep within your heart
A place apart
Where little dreams may go,
May thrive and grow.
Hold fast — hold fast your dreams!

— Louise Driscoll

You Can Do It

When life looks like a mountain that is impossible to climb, just remember how incredible you are.

You have all the resources you need to see you through. You have optimism and a graceful way of dealing with adversity.

You are a courageous person who has faced challenges before and always come bouncing back with a smile on your face. You are resilient and courageous, especially when you feel doubtful and uncertain. It is in these times that you show your true strength of character.

When life tests you, remember that you are so much bigger than you think you are. Your buoyant spirit will win once again. Whatever it takes, you can do it.

— Lynda Field

You've Got What It Takes

You may be feeling a little uncertain
about your future right now,
but you need to trust your decisions
    and feelings
and do what is best for you.
The future will work itself out;
you're the kind of person
who can make it happen.
Don't let anyone else's negativity
influence your dreams, values,
    or hopes.
Focus on what you can change
and let go of what you can't.
You know your own worth,
what you've accomplished,
and what you're capable of.

Your goals may take a bit longer
and be harder to achieve
than you had hoped,
but concentrate on the positives
and combine faith with
generous portions of patience
and determination.
Step boldly and confidently
    into your future
where happiness, success,
and dreams await you.

You have the potential
    for greatness...
never give up.
                        — Barbara Cage

What Does It Mean to Succeed?

Most people see success as being rich and famous or powerful and influential. Others see it as being at the top of their profession and standing out from the rest.

The wise see success in a more personal way; they see it as achieving the goals they have set for themselves, and then feeling pride and satisfaction in their accomplishments. True success is felt in the heart, not measured by money and power.

So be true to yourself and achieve the goals you set. For success is reaching those goals and feeling proud of what you have accomplished.

— Tim Tweedie

Success is not measured by how well
you fulfill the expectations of others,
but by how honestly you live up to
your own expectations.
When you are true to yourself
in the pursuit of your dream,
you have earned the right
to be proud of your accomplishment.

— Linda Principe

Success is in the way you walk
   the paths of life each day;
It's in the little things you do
   and in the things you say.
Success is in the glad hello
   you give your fellow man;
It's in the laughter of your home
   and all the joys you plan.

Success is not in getting rich
   or rising high to fame;
It's not alone in winning goals
   which all men hope to claim...

It's in the man you are each day,
    through happiness or care.
It's in the cheery words you speak
    and in the smile you wear.

Success is being big of heart
    and clean and broad of mind;
It's being faithful to your friends,
    and to the stranger, kind;
It's in the children whom you love,
    and all they learn from you —
Success depends on character
    and everything you do.

                    — Edgar A. Guest

The Seed of Greatness
Lies Within You

Believe in yourself
and your vision of the future.
Keep your dreams alive
despite the challenges
along the way.

There will always be those
who try to steal your dream
by laughter or criticism.
They cannot understand what
drives you to always want more.

In safety, there is no failure —
neither is there success.
Only by taking the risks
that others fear
can you achieve greatness.

Change can be frightening,
but only by changing
can you experience growth.
Only by challenging yourself
to do what seems impossible
can you ever know how much
you can achieve.

There is only one key to success:
never quit until you win.
It may require a lot of changing,
but you can do it.
The seed of greatness
lies within you.
Nurture it, and there
will be nothing you can't do.

— Lisa Marie Yost

The World Needs More Dreamers

Dreamers take chances.
Like everyone else, they fear failing,
but they refuse to let fear control them.
Dreamers don't give up.
When life gets rough, they hang in
    until the going gets better.
Dreamers are flexible.
They realize there is more than one way
    and are willing to try others.
Dreamers know they are not perfect.
They respect their weaknesses
while making the most of their strengths.
Dreamers fall, but they don't stay down.
They stubbornly refuse to let a fall
    keep them from climbing.

Dreamers don't blame fate for their failures
    nor luck for their successes.
Dreamers accept responsibility for their lives.
Dreamers are positive thinkers who see
    good in all things.
From the ordinary, they make the extraordinary.
Dreamers believe in the path they have chosen
    even when it's hard,
even when others can't see where they are going.
Dreamers are patient.
They know a goal is only as worthy
as the effort that's required to achieve it.

— Nancye Sims

When You Believe...
Anything Is Possible

Believe in what makes you feel good.
Believe in what makes you happy.
Believe in the dreams
    you've always wanted to come true,
        and give them every chance to.
Life holds no promises
    as to what will come your way.
You must search for your own ideals
    and work toward reaching them.
Life makes no guarantees
    as to what you'll have.
It just gives you time to make choices
    and to take chances
and to discover whatever secrets
    that might come your way.

If you are willing to take
    the opportunities you are given
        and utilize the abilities you have,
you will constantly fill your life
    with special moments
        and unforgettable times.
No one knows the mysteries of life
    or its ultimate meaning,
but for those who are willing
    to believe in their dreams
        and in themselves,
life is a precious gift
    in which anything is possible.

— Dena Dilaconi

Don't Ever Stop Dreaming Your Dreams

Don't ever try to understand everything —
    some things will just never make sense.
Don't ever be reluctant to show your feelings:
    When you're happy, give in to it!
    When you're not, live with it.
Don't ever be afraid to try to
    make things better —
    you might be surprised at the results.
Don't ever take the weight of the world
    on your shoulders.

Don't ever feel threatened by the future —
    take life one day at a time.
Don't ever feel guilty about the past —
    what's done is done. Learn from any
    mistakes you might have made.
Don't ever feel that you are alone —
    there is always somebody there for you
    to reach out to.
Don't ever forget that you can achieve
    so many of the things you can imagine —
    imagine that! It's not as hard as it seems.
Don't ever stop loving,
    don't ever stop believing,
        don't ever stop dreaming your dreams.
                                — Laine Parsons

Let Your Dreams Take You Wherever You Want to Go

Follow your dreams
and they will lead you to the road
that you were born to travel.

As you take the next step
in life's journey...
remember to always listen
to the voice inside your heart.

Believe in yourself —
because you are a very special person
with so many gifts and talents.

May the days that lie ahead
bring you all the happiness
and success that you deserve.

— Jason Blume

ACKNOWLEDGMENTS

We gratefully acknowledge the permission granted by the following authors and authors' representatives to reprint poems or excerpts from their publications.

Susan Polis Schutz for "If you know yourself well...," "Sometimes you may think...," "People Who Achieve Their Dreams Have Twelve Qualities in Common," "Always Believe in Yourself and Your Dreams," "Sometimes we do not feel...," and "You can have many dreams...." Copyright © 1982, 1986, 1988, 2003, 2013 by Stephen Schutz and Susan Polis Schutz. And for "It is so important...." Copyright © 1979 by Continental Publications. All rights reserved.

Jason Blume for "One Step at a Time" and "Let Your Dreams Take You Wherever You Want to Go." Copyright © 2005, 2013 by Jason Blume. All rights reserved.

PrimaDonna Entertainment Corp. for "I believe all of us have..." and "Reflect on all that you are..." by Donna Fargo. Copyright © 1996, 2005 by PrimaDonna Entertainment Corp. All rights reserved.

The Leading Edge Publishing Company, www.theleadingedgepublishing.com, for "Whatever you vividly imagine..." by Paul J. Meyer. Copyright © 1997 by Paul J. Meyer. All rights reserved.

A careful effort has been made to trace the ownership of selections used in this anthology in order to obtain permission to reprint copyrighted material and give proper credit to the copyright owners. If any error or omission has occurred, it is completely inadvertent, and we would like to make corrections in future editions provided that written notification is made to the publisher:

BLUE MOUNTAIN ARTS, INC., P.O. Box 4549, Boulder, Colorado 80306.